D0851782

Hard Love Province

ALSO BY MARILYN CHIN

Revenge of the Mooncake Vixen

Rhapsody in Plain Yellow

The Phoenix Gone, the Terrace Empty

Dwarf Bamboo

Hard Love Province

Poems

MARILYN CHIN

W. W. NORTON & COMPANY

New York · London

For information about permission to reproduce selections from this book,
write to Permissions, W. W. Norton & Company, Inc.,
500 Fifth Avenue, New York, NY 10110

For information about special discounts for bulk purchases, please contact
W. W. Norton Special Sales at specialsales@wwnorton.com or 800-233-4830

Manufacturing by Courier Westford
Production manager: Julia Druskin

ISBN 978-0-393-24096-2

W. W. Norton & Company, Inc.
500 Fifth Avenue, New York, N.Y. 10110
www.wwnorton.com

W. W. Norton & Company Ltd.
Castle House, 75/76 Wells Street, London W1T 3QT

1 2 3 4 5 6 7 8 9 0

The door itself
Makes no promises.

—ADRIENNE RICH

CONTENTS

III.

IV.

ACKNOWLEDGMENTS

I thank the editors of the following journals:

Poetry: selections from *Beautiful Boyfriend*

Northwest Review: Formosan Elegy

The New Republic: selections from *Nocturnes* and *Cougar Sinonymous*

The Iowa Review: Summer Sleep

Paterson Review: Alba

Parnassus: Twenty Five Haiku

Poets.org: *One Child Has Brown Eyes*

Ploughshares: Study Hall, Deterritorialized

Poet Lore: Costume Drama

Crate: The Great Escape

Prairie Schooner: Every Woman Is Her Own Chimera

Cimarron Review: Naked I Come, Naked I Go

Provincetown Arts: Horns

Meridians: Kalifornia

I thank the following foundations and institutions for their generous support: the Gaea Foundation (Sea Change residency), the United States Artists Foundation, the Rockefeller Foundation (residency at

Bellagio), the Radcliffe Institute for Advanced Studies at Harvard, the Stadler Center for Poetry at Bucknell University, the Headlands Center for the Creative Arts, Yaddo, and San Diego State University.

I **thank** the wise and kind Martha Collins who helped me reorder the splendid beast. I thank my valiant brother Bob Grunst who has been my faithful first reader for many years. I thank many friends and family members for their boundless generosity during my times of grief. A kiss of gratitude to sister poet Harriet Levin, brother poet Henri Cole, surrogate mother Dorothea Kehler.

I **thank** Jill Bialosky, sister writer and editor extraordinaire, for her continuous support. I thank Sandy Dijkstra, my inspiring agent, for her tireless encouragement. I thank the hardworking posses and girl gangs in both the W. W. Norton and S.D.L.A. offices . . . particularly, I want to shout out to Elise Capron and Andrea Cavallaro.

I **thank** Don Lonewolf Romero, my eternal love: our short life together was pure, unexpurgated joy!

Hard Love Province

I

Alba: Moon Camellia Lover

for Don Lonewolf

Last night through the camellia boles
I gazed, transfixed, at the moon—
Pale-faced, hook-nosed.
I know that she is my mother
Staring back from death, a dark matter.
For hours, we were one
With the earth's static blindness.
She did not envy the living
And I did not mourn the dead.
Tenderly, she lit up my face,
The camellia tree and my lover.
He, asleep on his side, cradling
His own soft sacks.

A few geese
Leave their noisy billows.
Home is a home away from home.
A neighbor's unfixed cat
Courting her own disaster.
A windless branch casts a hard silhouette
Certain of another tomorrow.

Suddenly, I witness the ecstasy of the changing hour—
As the sun devours the moon's corona
And the camellia unfurls

In brilliant pinks and reds, and my new love,
With a sweet smile on his sour lips
Struggles toward the bathroom.
His flanks are glistening pearls.

O my mother,
Let the sunlight erase your final torso.
Let the milk of all suffering
Fade into the traffic's clean hum.
Let father's white suit of sin
Blanch into my lover's swooning moans
And all be forgiven.
Let my happiness blister and counter-glow
Against your magnificent   sick   light.

Formosan Elegy

for Charles

You have lived six decades   and you have lived none
You have loved many   and you have loved no one
You wedded three wives   but you lie in your cold bed alone
You sired four children   but they cannot forgive you

Knock at emptiness   a house without your love
Strike the pine box   no answer   all hollow
You planted plums near the gate   but they bear no fruit
You raised herbs in the veranda   fresh and savory

I cry for you   but no sound wells up in my throat
I sing for you   but my tears have dried in my gullet
Walk the old dog   give the budgies a cool bath
Cut a tender melon   let it bleed into memory

The robe you washed   hangs like a carcass flayed
The mug you loved   is stained with old coffee
Your toothbrush is silent   grease mums your comb
Something's lost   something's made strong

Around the corner   a new prince yearns to be loved
A fresh turn of phrase   a bad strophe erased
A random image   crafts itself into a poem
A sleepless Taipei night   a mosquito's symphony

Who will cry for you   me and your sister Colette
Who will cry for you   me and your Algerian sister
You were a rich man   but you held on to your poverty
You were a poor man   who loved gold over dignity

I sit near your body bag   and sing you a last song
I sit near your body bag   and chant your final sutra
What's our place on earth?   nada   nada   nada
What's our destiny?   war   grief   maggots   nada

Arms   cheeks   cock   femur   eyelids   nada
Cowl   ox   lamb   vellum   marrow   nada
Vulva   nada   semen   nada   ovum   nada
Eternity   nada   heaven   nada   void   nada

Birth and death   the same blackened womb
Birth and death   the same white body bag
Detach   detach   we enter the world alone
Detach   detach   we leave the world bone lonely

If we can't believe in god   we must believe in love
We must believe in love   we must believe in love
And they zip you up   in your white body bag
White body bag   white   white   body   bag

Nocturnes

Beautiful moon   the murderer begins to sing
   The thief takes off his mask   to smell   the heliotrope

A dirty girl's face   against a clear night pane
   Dreams of a strawberry pie   at Marie Callender's

A junkie steals asters from a rich man's grave
   And spreads them   on the modest mound of his mother

A lone girl walks with moonlit haste   in the shadow of
   the *maquiladoras*

❖

Pol Pot sleeps   counting heaven's lambs
   His ex-wife is learning ikebana

The pine and the pagoda   so perfectly displaced
   She ponders the beauty   of the symmetrical

❖

A pretty boy dances naked in a cage
Twelve or thirteen   he is brown and slender
He sings   *My father sold me to the hillside wolves*
For a snort of the white dragon

❖

He sings   *Let me return to die*
In the land of fish and sugarcane
Where the boys are golden and the girls are wry
In the land of fish and sugarcane

❖

Wild Boar gnaws   on the boy's pretty face
    The boy gnaws   on pork tripe dumplings
Wild Boar savors   the boy's rotting stench
    The boy loves   his fragrant pork dumplings

The dead boy wades   face down in marl
    The dead boar's snout   points toward heaven
Lotus blooms   in the lord's cosmic soup
    To forgive   the eater and the eaten

❖

The sky does not judge   it's black and starless
    The geese squawking high   plot their destination

The Goddess   sprawls   on a cool chaise lounge
    Feeds grapes   to her young paramour

❖

The corpse of my love   reappears in a dream
    The corpse of my love   unzips his own body bag

His scarlet hand is turning brilliant green
    His purple heart   *tin tin na bu lations!*

❖

A mask on horseback   is not your friend
    A mask on horseback   is not your savior

Run little sister beyond   the rabbit-proof fence
    As far as your skinny legs take you

❖

Buddha cannot save you   he's detached   detached
    Christ hates himself   and other Jews in his image

No eternity   in the land you love
    Only eternal   the suffering

❖

What is democracy   but too many things
    And too little time to love them

Cut up my body   rearrange my face
    Jackdaws   mole crickets   I am not afraid of you

❖

Every blossom   breaks my heart
    Every leaf falls   into memory

Every raindrop   cries on the shanty roof
    A streak of moonlight   blinds me

❖

The fat man of love is dead   Pavarotti and Barry White are
        dead
The fat man of love is dead   dead   dead!
Israel K   Alas!   Alas!

The fat man of love is dead   Elvis   dead   dead!
And the thin man   Sinatra   croons all night long
    Dead   dead   my maidenhead!

❖

The monkey claps and claps   his cymbals are tired
Prosperity   decline   what does it matter?
We will wind down this year   and slump over

❖

A deathblow is life blow to some
    Tell them   Emily   those woolly ministers

Chopin's fingers play   soft   soft   soft
    Comforting   the   beasts   and   flowers

Summer Sleep (after Meng Haoran)

for Donald Justice

Summer sleep   I missed the dawn
My tired eyes   too heavy to open

Far off birds argue   freeways hiss
Car alarms trill   false emergencies

In dream I am ten   napping in the Master's house
My single bed   a one-girl coffin

Too tight! I cry   *my feet can't fit!*
He scowls and sighs   scorns my mediocrity

Rain dances   death coins on the roof
Time devours us   imperceptibly

Empty womb   pupils beg for entry
Unfinished poems   don't know how many

Twenty Five Haiku

❖

A hundred red fire ants scouring, scouring the white peony

❖

Fallen plum blossoms return to the branch, you sleep, then
    harden again

❖

Cuttlefish in my palm stiffens with rigor mortis, boy toys can't
    love

❖

Neighbor's barn: grass mat, crickets, Blue Boy, trowel handle,
    dress soaked in mud

❖

Iron-headed mace, double-studded halberd slice into emptiness

❖

O fierce Oghuz, tie me to two wild elephants, tear me in half

❖

O my swarthy herder, two-humped bactrian, drive me the long
    distance

❖

Forceps, tongs, *bushi*, whip, flanks, scabbard, stirrup, goads,
    distaff, wither, awl

❖

Black-eyed Susans, Queen Anne's lace, bounty of cyclamen,
    mown paths erupt

❖

Gaze at the charred hills, the woebegone kiosks, we are all
    God's hussies

❖

I have not fondled the emperor's lapdog, whose name is Black
    Muzzle

❖

Urge your horses into the mist-swilled Galilee, O sweet
    Bedlamite

❖

Her Majesty's randying up the jewel stairs to find the pleasure
    dome

❖

Ancient pond: the frog jumps in and in and in, the deep slap of
    water

❖

The frog jumps into the ancient pond: she says, no, I am not
     ready

❖

Coyote cooked his dead wife's vagina and fed it to his new wife

❖

I plucked out three white pubic hairs and they turned into
     flying monkeys

❖

Let's do it on the antimacassar, on the antimacassar

❖

Little Red drew her teeny pistol from her basket and said "eat
     me"

❖

Chimera: Madame Pol Pot grafting a date tree onto a date tree

❖

His unworthy appendage, his mutinous henchman grazed my
     pink cheeks

❖

He on top now changes to bottom, Goddess welcomes her
     devotee

❖

Fish fish fowl fowl, mock me Mistress Bean Curd, I am both
　　duck and essence

❖

Don't touch him, bitch, we're engaged; and besides, he's
　　wearing my nipple ring

❖

Sing sing little yellow blight rage rage against the dying of the
　　light

II

One Child Has Brown Eyes

One child has brown eyes, one has blue
One slanted, another rounded
One so nearsighted he squints internal
One had her extra epicanthic folds removed
One downcast, one couldn't be bothered
One roams the heavens for a perfect answer
One transfixed like a dead doe, a convex mirror
One shines double-edged like a poisoned dagger
Understand their vision, understand their blindness
Understand their vacuity, understand their mirth

Study Hall, Deterritorialized

(for Gwendolyn Brooks)

The brown boy hits me, but says he is sorry. The brown girl, his sister, says it's because he likes me. I say, *yuk! He likes me? Well, I hate him.* The black girl pinches me and says, *Scaredy-cat, tattletale, little pussy, I dare you to hit back.* The white girl grabs my Hello Kitty purse and spills my milk money. I karate-chop her arm. The white boy says, *My father says that your father's egg rolls are made of fried rat penises.* I answer, *Yep, my father says that the reason why his egg rolls are made of fried rat penises is because Americans are weirdos and like to eat fried rat penises.* The black girl laughs deep from her gut and high-fives me. Just as I am redrawing the map, my little fresh-off-the-boat cousin from Malaysia starts weeping into her pink shawl like a baby, *wa wa wa.* The white girl muffles her ears, *Can't you shut her up?*

I say, *Don't cry, little cousin, it's not as bad as it seems. It's verse!* I point to the window and magically, to entertain us, two fat pigeons appear cooing on the sill. The boy is sitting on top of the girl, trying to molest her. She is wobbling, shuffling, pirouetting under his weight. He is pecking a red, bald spot on her skinny neck and singing:

> *We real cooooool   we real foooools . . .*
> *We real cooooool   we real foooools . . .*

Finally, we all laugh as one, laughing and laughing at God's beloved creatures. Behind this spectacle, against all odds, from the west, a strong explosion of sun bullies through the big-gray-loogie-of-a-cloud.

Costume Drama

for Adrienne Rich

Tamra's bawling into her burka: she misses her mother
   Paulie's growling into his cowl
   Oh, stuff it, says Nellie, it's not cool

Misha's sniffling into his yashmak, meanwhile, yakety-yak
   German's chewing on his chiton

Ritta blows her nose into her babushka
   Says, "You have problems with that?"
   Homi's unraveling his dhoti
   Stephanie's wheezing into her chemise
   Gozo's slouching in his happi coat

Fong just soiled her sarong, tries to get to the bathroom
   But the line's too long
Danny tears up his Yankee jersey, says
   "I hate you all, I wanna go home!"

The Great Matriarch says
   "Snot-nosed little terrorists! I know what you've done
   You are all guilty!"

Cougar Sinonymous

My grandpa was eighty   my grandma was twenty
She cried for years   for the good life she was missing
She faced the wall   until he finished his dying
Then she polished his bones   for all of eternity

❖

Such entitlement   my prickly little prince
Waving a pistol   and a crumpled Ben Franklin
Don't you know   I'm a citizen of my own bed?
I paid for my passage   I owe you nothing

❖

Throw my girl into the river   she won't drown
Like her mother before her   and her mother's mother
Stubborn reed   hollow at both ends
She'll whistle and hum   and float into dawn

❖

The man from Worcester   wants to eat my sister
He bends her backward   coats her in rice flour
Pinches her corners   calls her "sweet dumpling"
Fries her in deep oil   then serves her on porcelain

❖

Who is the Buddha   a shit-wiping gumstick
Who is the Buddha   a painter's triptych
Who is the Buddha   he is naked   utterly naked
Who is the Buddha   a stele   a herdboy   a sweet nothing

❖

When I saw his corpse   I knew he was mine
A flash of kerosene   epaulets   cheap aftershave
His flesh burnt black   his mouth agape
Silently shouting   another woman's name

❖

How sweet   someone else's husband
Lurking around   the girls' gymnasium
How sweet   someone else's student
Tanned and arrogant   reciting bad poems

❖

A flower   and yet not a flower
A dream   and yet not a dream
At midnight   he comes to my bed
At daylight   he returns to the dead

❖

Hold on to your boy soldier on the moonlit path
I am an urban cougar on the sunset prowl
Once I take his nape in my bloody mouth
He'll beg and moan and succumb to God

❖

His loveroot dangling   before a crimson sac
His tresses long   disheveled   and raven black
My warrior my warrior   mounting a tall horse
My thighbird is calling   she wants you back

❖

My cousin calls him Allah   my sister calls him Jesus
My brother calls him Krishna   my mother calls him Gautama
I call him call him   on his cell phone
But he does not answer

❖

I climb the Acropolis   swim in the Aegean
Flirt with Kouros   but don't give him my name
Drink tea at high noon   eat octopus at dusk
A woman at forty   is proud of her lust

❖

She mounted a proud white steed
A proud white steed mounted she
Of late she preferred a dapple-gray, a roan, a sorrel, a motley bay
And a randy war pony was he

❖

Hell no   Dude-bro!   You think you own this poetry
I see your lips trembling   counting syllables
Cry epiphany   long before   the penultimate turn
A dry cough   and a verse   smears the ceiling

❖

Pretty poem   pretty poem   pretty poem
A nosegay of poesies
Pretty boy   pretty boy   supine and lazy
Die a third time   we'll pen you an elegy

❖

What they say about a woman at forty-five
Too late to live   too soon to die
My wine is bittersweet   my song is wry
My yoni still tight   my puma is on fire

Sonnetnese (after Su Tong Po)

Ugly wives and bitchy concubines
they are one and the same

The blacker the black coffee   the more I want two cups
All I get in Beijing is shit Nescafé   sugary muck
Beauty / ugliness   selfsame skyline   obscured by smog
Imperial killjoy   drunk on his back   can't get it up
I love socialist architecture!   flabby husbands   alcoholic hard
      bucks
The sadder they get   the more I love them   I can't get
      enough
You could be a rich corpse   or a poor corpse
Stuff all your cavities   with jade and river pearls   powdery
      gold snuff
The robbers will pluck them   like fragrant florets
Silly boy   eyes closed   puckered   you wait for love
Gripe about how life has cheated you   of fame   of riches
End of a violent century   you are nostalgic for blood
My dear   we are staring at the void   at the edge of
      Americanness
The begonia is too beautiful   we must love   and be loved

October Song

The prince speaks

Let me lower the curtains, my love
    Our last night together is brief
Let me straighten our wedding quilt
    And warm it for you, my love

Let me fold your nightgown, my love
    Let me unfasten your hair
Let me lift the veil from your face
    To see my bride's last cry

Heaven is our starry canopy, my love
    Earth is our eternal bed
Let us drift in our cold black railroad car
    And wake to empire again

The Great Escape

One day in court, my Great-Great-Uncle Wu the bailiff broke wind. Lord Yuan said, "Who has shown contempt? Bring the perpetrator before me!" His subjects all laughed, some rattled their irons, some squealed in their cangues. Wu said, "I'm sorry, sire, the culprit has fled. I saw the long tail of his gilded robe fly through the eastern gate. But, I shall corner him in the royal stables, he shall meet his fate."

So, Uncle Wu went to the stables and found a fresh turd, wrapped it in vermilion silk, stamped it with a paraffin seal and displayed it on a jade plate. "Your Honor, I am afraid that the culprit has escaped, but I have managed to collect one of his relatives." And for this piece of too-late-in-the-empire buffoonery, Lord Yuan pulled out his sword from its ornate scabbard and lopped off Wu's head.

From a Notebook of an Ex-Revolutionary

I pierced my nose once and bled
It scummed and scabbed and bled
I pierced a new hole and bled
It scummed and scabbed and bled
The infection refused to give
It scummed and scabbed and bled

❖

White picket fence
 A red chicken

Ain't my people's imagism

❖

The urinal is perfect
NOT!

❖

I dreamt that I was naked save a pair of designer stilettos and was
ruthlessly networking at a benefit soiree. Suddenly, I was cata-
pulted into the midst of strangling this famous court poet. I tried
to deflect my scandalous action by arguing with the freckled-
faced bartender. "What kind of a Virgin Mary is this: where
is the Tabasco? Whence the celery stick?" I watched the world
shrink into a penlight: how frail the court poet's neck, how small
this poetry world. Meanwhile, an ex-student, an up-and-coming

famous court poet, upchucked on my shoes! I shouted, "God-damn, not on my brand-new faux Pradas. If you're going to gen-uflect, do it before the porcelain Madonna!" To soothe myself, I sang a short ditty: *Poor little rice-girl, little rice-girl. Surely, the hem of privilege is soaked with crud.*

❖

Auntie Wu said to Michelangelo Wong, "How can you paint the Buddha so goodly and beget so foul of children?"
Michelangelo Wong replied, "I paint the temple in daylight and make my children in the dark."

❖

(HARD LABOR)

Jon Yi was born in the caves of Yenan,
Did the Long March on his mother's breast.
He grew up and became a Red Guard,
Placed a dunce cap on the very same mother,
Marched her to Xinjiang, to die of hard labor.

Twenty years later in Sonoma California
He confessed to his loving wife—I'm a weakling.
A spineless scoundrel, a turtle's spawn.
A lackey, a whelp-dog.   He squealed and squealed,
History made me do it! History made me do it!

❖

(DUELING QUATRAINS)

> *Sylvia*
> You baked me a cake   and it's not even my birthday
> I ate a slice politely   though it's wormy and stale
> How thin   you are   dear Sylvia   how terribly thin
> You must be suffering from poetry

> *Emily*
> Eternity suits you   Emily   new rouge on your cheeks
> *Entertainment Today*   wants to interview you
> How Mr. So and So Higginson   spurned your love
> How Mr. So and So Johnson   mended your bones

❖

> The ash fell all day today
>   Fell all day yesterday
> Will fall all day tomorrow
>   From Dachau to Buchenwald

> From the Pripyat River
>   To the Kiev Reservoir
> From the Fukushima shores
>   To the Tōdai-ji temple

One bonshō bell
    Cries out to

Another

And   a
            lame   ox
Goes
        vir
            al

Black President

If a black man could be president
Could a white man be his slave?
Could a sinner enter heaven
By uttering his name?

If the terminator is my governor
Could a cowboy be my king?
When shall the cavalry enter Deadwood
And save my prince?

An exo-cannibal eats her enemies
An indo-cannibal eats her friends
I'd rather starve myself silly
Than to make amends

Blood on the altar   Blood on the lamb
Blood in the chalice
Not symbolic   but fresh

III

Every Woman Is Her Own Chimera

A suite for Adrienne Rich

Every woman is her own chimera
Today she is laughing with Julio
Tonight she is dancing with Coolio

❖

How long can happiness last?
For a slow brief afternoon
My head on the thigh of a sequoia
Reading Wang Wei

❖

Butterfly in mouth
    But don't bite down
Whose life is it anyway?
    She born of chrysalis and shit
Or she born of woman and pain?

❖

Mei Ling brings a wounded poem
Crying   *Please Mommy   Mommy   fix it!*
You wipe the tears from her cheeks
Then glue a gnat's torn wing

❖

The sand dab flicks her tail
    The tears of the wombat are green
Kiss me against the last hydrangea
    Comrades we are not yet free

❖

O sunlit *bourrée* of doves
    O moonlit cantata of red ribbon
Let's drum girls   let's ululate   let's praise
    The White-Haired Maiden

❖

The Black Hawk scats   *vilip vilip vilip*
The Humvee murmurs   *surruu surruu*
Jackdaws boogie-down   *flip-flap flip-flap*
Marvin sighing   *mercy mercy mercy*

❖

All   I   want   is   love
My heart   my soul   my vulva
Yowl   *love love love*

❖

Look at him preen at the mirror
This aging retro-sexual
Combing combing his cowlick
In search of a perfect syllable

❖

Everybody's pregnant today
Even my cousin Louie
But cousin Louie is a man
Yes everybody's pregnant today
Even my cousin Louie

❖

Ax is chopping down Tree
Tree begs Ax to stop
Your handle is made of wood
We are born from the same mother

❖

A pink horse is not a horse
A pink horse is not a horse
A pink horse is not a horse
A pink horse is not a horse

❖

They will shave your head
Send you to the colonies
A brown man's musket
Will shoot you dead
He must defend his dignity

Do not do not believe in eternity

❖

Poke me with an idle chopstick
I am mum as a flayed *ebi*
Bored with judgment and hate
And tired of pity

❖

We must not be silenced
        Yet
                We are
Silenced

Brush
        returning
  to

VOID

❖

It's not that you are rare
Nor are you extraordinary

O lone wren sobbing on the bodhi tree
You are simple and sincere

Brown Girl Manifesto (Too)

Metaphor   metaphor   my pestilential aesthetic
    A tsunami powers through   my mother's ruins
Delta   delta   moist loins of the republic
    Succumb to the low-lying succubus   do!

Flagpole   flagpole   my father's polemics
    A bouquet of   fuck-u-bastard flowers
Fist me   embrace me   with your phantom limbs
    Slay me   with your slumlord   panegyrics

Flip over   so I can see your pastoral mounts
    Your sword   slightly parting from the scabbard
Girl skulls   piled like fresh baked loaves
    A foul wind   scours my mother's cadaver

Ornamental   Oriental   techno   impresarios
    I am your parlor rug   your chamber bauble
Love me   stone me   I am all yours
    Pound   Pound   my father's Ezra

Freedom   freedom   flageolet-tooting girls
Dancing   on the roof   of the *maquiladoras*

Kalifornia (A portrait of the poet wearing a girdle of severed heads)

Marilyn Mei Ling Chin
You are a Goddess
You beautiful swine
You necklace of heads
You girdle of past deeds

You have a castle
With a vestibule
You have your fresh lovers
O how you wear them like nipple rings

You have your listlessness
Its dull ache
You have your fine breasts
Your hard maids

You have your strong presences
Better than absences
Better than abscesses
You have your coital fire

Behold, Great Mother
Your black rope of hair

Behold: breasts, crotch
Scrotum, harbor, sun

Your poems will write themselves on parchment
Your manuscripts will illuminate
Any moment now
The diasporas will form a new dialect

Your tears will turn into saltlick
You can walk forever naked
On the island of Caucausus
Without harm

You have your disciples
Tanned and ephemeral
You have your death
The inevitable long drive

They will paint you black
They will paint you white
They will paint your yoni attached
To his blue lingam

Refute that a woman's body
    Is impure
Refute that a woman's body
    Is filthy

Although a woman's body
   Is filthy
They adorn you with garlands

If God is a woman
Why does the world remain
Smug
And male?

Slouched on the blue-cloud divan
The lord of sleep
Flips the channels
Of conscience

A clapboard city in flames
A thousand arms of the marauders
Lowered again, again
On a bloodied cranium

If you hate
There will be a smoldering silence
If you love
There will also be
A purifying furnace

For poetry makes nothing happen
It survives in the Bethesda Boys
Of its making
Where bankers tweet on boughs

And Humvees on their backs
Pray for transcendence

You have a surfeit of choices
You have no choice
A boon of blood-red hibiscus
Stains the burial grounds

The hurly-gurly orphan bands chant
Reverence to her
Reverence to her
And your flesh ignites
Into screams

IV

Two Inch Fables

A tiny droplet fell on a lotus pad
She pranced and rolled like a precious pearl
I am perfect   I am unique
God made me and tossed the mold
Then a blast of gale pushed her over
The edge of the waxy frond
She plunged down the murky depths
Into the dirty   duck-shit   of oblivion

❖

I love my beautiful vulva
Vulva   vulva   vulva
It shines like a brilliant peach
And tremors with dazzling dew
I fear my poem is too vulgar
So I change my "vulva" to "nova"
Now I love my beautiful nova
It explodes into the great unknown

❖

I am an ass   the Master said
I am the ass's buttocks
I am the ass's feces   one rejoined
I am the maggot on the feces
And what were you doing there

O lowliest of the low?
I was enjoying summer vacation

❖

Tear the fly from the flypaper, let him die
Take the roach out of the motel, let him fly
The dead dingle on the fence makes amends
Free the cock from sacrifice, free the hen
Let the orphans feed, set the widows free
Teach a killer how to cry
We must love one another or die
Love one another or die

❖

One persimmon, two persimmon the third has ripened
So juicy and sweet, we must not waste love

Two persimmon, three persimmon, the fourth has ripened
We must eat it soon, our last chance for enlightenment

Three persimmon, four persimmon, the fifth is rotten
Too bad, you waited too long

Ditty's become a dirge
Mocking our impermanence

❖

Baby, you're a cheap thrill
A dinner buys surrender

A Long Island iced tea makes you tipsy
Nothing so bittersweet
As a boy so tender
I'll keep you warm in my sheath
My mojo is my love shield
The Huns are stirring the pot
Chanting boystew   boystew   boystew

❖

We met south of the painted wall
He unzipped his soiled chiton
I kept my black thong on
He kissed me hard against the column
And bruised my arm
Let's die, let's die now
The Mongols are close on the path
And there's no tomorrow

❖

All the world is filthy
I alone am clean
I alone am sober
All my homegirls are stoned

All the world is dancing
I alone am still
Lotuses   assemble   abstractly
Choking   the crystal   clear   pond

❖

The scabbard is chafing your thigh
The yoke is digging into your nape
The cangue is rubbing you raw
Baby, cut off your queue
Your coolie days are over
This late capitalist immigrant bitch
Will ransom your pretty ass home

❖

She is headless and armless
He is missing a topknot
She still poised for victory
He, valor and faithfulness

A wing broken, a nose detached
She marble, he terracotta
They shall stand lonely on that pedestal
Long after the aftermath

❖

Crow squats in the road
Pecking on a recent kill
Canary is high on a branch
Singing for her supper
Crow says: My, you are a pretty bird
Pretty bird, pretty bird
Who will hand-feed you now
Not your lord, my cadaver!

❖

Yellow gold is meaningless
Learning is better than pearls
A woman without brilliance
Leaves nothing but dim children

You can hawk your gold if you're hungry
Sell your mule when you're desperate
What can you do with so many poems
Sprouting dead hairs in an empty coffin

❖

Lotus: pink   dewlapped   pretty
Lotus: upturned palm of my dead mother
Lotus: a foot   a broken arch
Lotus: plop   and a silent   ripple

❖

I hum and stroll
And contemplate a poem
While young boys are dying
In West Darfur

I hum and stroll
And contemplate a poem
While young boys are dying
In West Darfur

❖

Gwen came down from heaven
Baked me a sweet potato pie
June's stirring rice pudding
Gives me the stink eye
Sylvia says
Girl poet you ain't worth the bacon
Just wipe the blood from the oven
Go home! Go home!

❖

Dog   if you bite   bite gently
Cat if you scratch   find my funny bone
Fly   kiss my eyes twice   then summon
Your brethren

Wolf   drag my bones slowly
Keep me whole
For another summer
Vulture
I am not afraid of your leavings

❖

Eng says to Chang: Oh let's love with a single heart
Let's die in eternal embrace and never part
Ritta says to Christina: we have two heads and one pussy
We are doomed to eternal misery
Vinnie says to Emily

Do we have two souls or just one?
Or are you just a shadow sister and love no one?

❖

I am a lonely Chinese poet
Sitting on the nether ridge
You are a Ute Mountain warrior
The sun has begun to set

❖

What is the Buddha?
Two pounds of ground turkey
What is the Buddha?
Oh she broke a fingernail
What is the Buddha?
A Haitian girl and a Laotian girl
What is the Buddha?
She's b-boying at the bus stop

❖

I am a gold lock
            You are a gold key
I am a brass lock
            You are a brass key
I am a skeleton lock
            You are a skeleton key
I am a monk lock

You are a monkey
Ha ha ha ha!

❖

(for Denise Levertov)

So, you're going to Black Mountain
Black Mountain so far
Black Mountain so unreachable
So you will meet Snyder and Rauschenberg
And Cage and his zenny music
At Black Mountain
And so shall you love a Goodman
There

❖

Flowers blossom on her back
Tendrils wrap his withered thigh
Melilotus dangling on her brow ridge
Clover covers his fingernails

Because the truth is so very   very   sad
Oh anonymous corpse in the churchyard
I must dream of you
                    festooned with flowers

Naked I Come, Naked I Go

for Ai

I take off my antique Navajo turquoise
Pull off my red cashmere sweater
Wiggle out of my black leather jeans, Lord, they've been tight!

I wipe off my kohl eye shadow and plum lip gloss
I free my hair from my mother-of-pearl comb
I put on my original face

I walk away from my small rented prairie house
I climb into my last yellow taxi
Oh trusted pony, take me home!

Horns: A Coda

During the tenth month of the first year of the reign of Emperor Jing, a little girl from the southernmost province of Guangdong grew horns. The horns were hideously sharp with little tufts of greenish hair sprouting in the ridges. When the new emperor heard about this monster, he ordered his five most valiant soldiers to execute her. But, when the soldiers arrived, the girl's grandmother had already sent her into the hills. The old woman, then, with proper demeanor, served the men last year's inferior crop of high mountain tea and quoted "The Book of Changes." *When an evil minister of state usurps power, the indigenes will grow horns.* The head soldier replied with a quick couplet from "The Treatise of the Five Monarchs." *Little girls, no matter how mistreated or angry, must not grow horns. Feudal citizens, no matter how unhappy, must not revolt against the lord.* Whereupon, he took out his sword and slayed the grandmother and mounted her head on a pole, as a warning to other renegade villagers.

Centuries of chaos and pogroms followed. Finally, rebellions were quashed, marauders were executed and there were no more incidents of little girls growing horns. By now, most of the world's citizens have smooth, unfurrowed hairlines. Albeit there was a sighting of a pair of razor-sharp growths erupting on the forehead of a little brown girl. She was last seen in the autumn of 2010, smooching with her surfer-dude boyfriend and strolling on a sun-flooded promenade in San Diego.

Beautiful Boyfriend

for Don (1958–2011)

My skiff is made of spicewood   my oars are Cassia bract
Music flows   from bow to starboard
Early Mozart   cool side of Coltrane   and miles and miles
          of Miles
Cheap Californian Merlot   and my new boyfriend

❖

My beautiful boyfriend   please shave your head
At the Miramar barbershop   take the tonsure
Bow toward the earth   prostrate and praise
Breathe in the Goddess's   potent citron

❖

Bullet   don't shoot him   he's my draft-horse
Night scope don't pierce him   he's my love-stalk
Sniper   who are you   high on the roof
Stop for a slow cigarette   let him escape

❖

If I could master   the nine doors of my body
And close my heart   to the cries of suffering
Perhaps   I could love you like no other
Float my mind   toward the other side of hate

❖

The shantytowns of Tijuana   sing for you
The slums of Little Sudan   hold evening prayer
One dead brown boy is a tragedy
    Ten thousand is a statistic
So let's fuck   my love   until the dogs pass

❖

All beautiful boyfriends are transitory
They have no souls   they're shiny brown flesh
Tomorrow they'll turn into   purple festering corpses
Fissured   gored   by myriad flies

❖

My boyfriend drives up   in his late Humvee
Says: *We're going to   hunt bin Laden*
We'll sleep in caves   and roast wild hare
And rise to praise   the bright red sun

❖

I was once   a beloved spotted ox
Now I've become   a war-horse of hate
I pulled the lorries   of ten thousand corpses
Before   I myself   was finally flayed

❖

Down the Irrawaddy River   you lay yourself to sleep
No sun   no moon   no coming   no going

No causality   no personality
No hunger   no thirst

❖

Skyward   beyond Angkor Wat
   Beyond   Jokhang Lhasa
You were floating   on a giant stupa
   Waiting   for   Our   Lord

❖

Malarial deltas   typhoidal cays
Tsunamis don't judge   calamity grieves no one
The poor will be submerged   the rich won't be saved
Purge the innocent   sink the depraved

❖

You push down my hand   with your bony hand
The fox-hair brush   lifts and bends
There's no revision in this life   you sigh
One bad stroke   and all is gone

❖

What do I smell   but the perfume of transience
Crushed calyxes   rotting phloems
Let's write   pretty poems   pretty poems   pretty poems
Mask stale pogroms   with a sweet whiff of oblivion

❖

Three shots into the wind   according to the rites
Heaven's stealth caissons   confess nothing
Lotus cannot cry   Buddha feels no pain
Surrender   you must   to one love   one nation

Goodbye

I asked him where he was heading this ungodly hour.
He said   *Don't nag me*   *Mei Ling*   *I am tired*
I am very very tired

I am going to rest in those southern hills
Don't bother calling   *I've disconnected my cell*
I'll tweet from the other side when I'm ready

I waved at the road until his bumper vanished
The traffic flowed toward eternity as my eyes teared up
Better stop crying he'll call me a sissy

Quiet the Dog, Tether the Pony

Gaze   gaze   beyond the vermilion door
Leaf   leaf   tremble   fall
Stare blankly   at the road's   interminable end

Reduplications   cold   cold   mountains
Long   long   valleys   broad   broad   waters
Tears   are exhausted   now   shed   blood

Deep   deep   the baleful courtyards   who knows how deep
Folds on folds   of curtains
Gates   trap   infinite   twilight

Walk   walk   through   waning meadows
Steep   steep   toward   ten thousand Buddhas
Knuckles   blue   on the balustrade

In the land of   missing   pronouns
Sun   is a   continuous   performance
And we   my love   are   nothing